SPEEDY FALCONS

by Bryan Langdo

Minneapolis, Minnesota

Credits

Cover and title page, © Boris Droutman/500px/Getty Images and © AlexanderLipko/Shutterstock; 5, © Harry Collins/Adobe Stock Images; 6–7, © Chris/Adobe Stock Images; 9, © Steve Oehlenschlager/Adobe Stock Images; 11, © Dagmara Ksandrova/Shutterstock; 12–13, © Dave Hutchison/Adobe Stock Images; 14, © MattCuda/iStock; 15, © scott mirror/Shutterstock; 17, © blickwinkel/Alamy Stock Photo; 18, © BoukeAtema/iStock; 19, © Nature Picture Library/ Alamy Stock Photo; 20, © Oscar Dominguez/Alamy Stock Photo; 20–21, © Richardom/ Alamy Stock Photo; 22TR, © McevoyKM/Shutterstock; 22ML, © Wirestock/iStock; 22BR, © Michael K. McDermott/Shutterstock; 23, © Kirk Wester/iStock

Bearport Publishing Company Product Development Team

Publisher: Jen Jenson; Director of Product Development: Spencer Brinker; Editorial Director: Allison Juda; Editor: Cole Nelson; Editor: Tiana Tran; Production Editor: Naomi Reich; Art Director: Kim Jones; Designer: Kayla Eggert; Designer: Steve Scheluchin; Production Specialist: Owen Hamlin

Statement on Usage of Generative Artificial Intelligence

Bearport Publishing remains committed to publishing high-quality nonfiction books. Therefore, we restrict the use of generative AI to ensure accuracy of all text and visual components pertaining to a book's subject. See BearportPublishing.com for details.

Library of Congress Cataloging-in-Publication Data is available at www.loc.gov or upon request from the publisher.

ISBN: 979-8-89577-059-7 (hardcover)
ISBN: 979-8-89577-176-1 (ebook)

Copyright © 2026 Bearport Publishing Company. All rights reserved. No part of this publication may be reproduced in whole or in part, stored in any retrieval system, or transmitted in any form or by any means, electronic, mechanical, photocopying, recording, or otherwise, without written permission from the publisher. Bearport Publishing is a division of FlutterBee Education Group.

For more information, write to Bearport Publishing, 3500 American Blvd W, Suite 150, Bloomington, MN 55431.

CONTENTS

Death from Above 4

Ruthless Raptors. 6

Worldly Birds 8

Sharp Eyes 10

Fierce Speed. 12

Terrifying Talons 14

Falcon Families 16

Protective Parents 18

Tiny Terrors. 20

Meet the Birds. 22
Glossary 23
Index 24
Read More 24
Learn More Online. 24
About the Author. 24

DEATH FROM ABOVE

As a falcon soars through the sky, it spots a smaller bird flying below. The fierce hunter folds back its thin wings and dives. The smaller bird tries to get away, but there is no escape from the **raptor**. The speeding falcon hits the bird with its feet, knocking it out. Then, the falcon flies away with its meal.

In addition to other birds, a falcon's **prey** includes insects, mice, and snakes.

RUTHLESS RAPTORS

Raptors, also known as birds of prey, are some of the most-skilled hunters in the animal kingdom. As **apex predators**, these birds hunt other animals without having to worry about being hunted themselves. Raptors track down their meals using amazing eyesight. They rip through the flesh of their prey with sharp **talons** and hooked beaks.

The word *raptor* comes from a word meaning to take away by force.

Eagles are some of the most well-known raptors.

WORLDLY BIRDS

Falcons speed across the skies over every continent except Antarctica. They live along coasts, over prairies and deserts, and in dense jungles. These terrors of the sky come in a range of sizes. The largest falcons have wingspans more than 4 feet (1.2 m) wide, while the smallest falcon has a wingspan that is only about 20 inches (53 cm) across.

Female falcons are usually bigger and stronger than males.

A peregrine falcon has a wingspan of 3.5 ft. (1 m).

SHARP EYES

Falcons have huge, powerful eyes that take up half of their skulls. They use their incredible eyesight to watch for prey while they perch in high places or glide through the sky. The birds can spot even small animals from up to 2 miles (3.2 km) away. Then, these skilled predators dive into action.

Falcons have eyes that face forward. This helps them focus on their prey.

FIERCE SPEED

Falcons have pointed wings with slim feathers that help the birds fly fast. Some falcons attack by tucking their wings close to their bodies and then dipping into a dive called a **stoop**. This allows them to travel at more than 200 miles per hour (322 kmh). **Translucent** eyelids protect their eyes from drying out as they shoot through the air.

A falcon's skull has special bones that hold their eyes in place during stoops.

A falcon can dive much faster than it can fly.

TERRIFYING TALONS

If its prey is flying, a falcon will curl its feet like fists and strike the creature in a mid-air dive. This attack will stun—and sometimes kill—the other bird. The fierce raptor then turns in the air and grabs its victim as it falls. For prey on the ground, a falcon will often fly by and scoop up the creature with its razor-sharp talons.

Falcons have smaller talons than most raptors.

If a creature survives the initial grab, a falcon uses its beak to snap the animal's spine!

FALCON FAMILIES

Falcons usually live alone except when it is time to **mate**. Then, the birds will find the same partner every year. The male digs a small pit where the female lays between two and five eggs. The female then sits on the eggs to **incubate** them while her partner brings her food.

Falcons dig their pit nests into cliffsides, sometimes making the homes perched as high as 1,300 ft. (396 m) off the ground!

PROTECTIVE PARENTS

After about a month, falcon hatchlings emerge from the eggs. Their parents keep an eye out for hungry predators, such as crows, owls, and even other falcons. Luckily for the chicks, their fierce parents are highly protective. To keep their young safe, falcon parents will screech and dive at any other bird that flies nearby.

Falcons will even sometimes attack humans who come too close to their chicks.

TINY TERRORS

Before young falcons can leave the nest, they do lots of flapping to make their wings strong. They take their first flight about four to seven weeks after they hatch and begin working on their hunting skills soon after. Within a few weeks, these young terrors take off from their nest for the last time to hunt the skies on their own.

A young saker falcon practices flapping its wings.

A young peregrine falcon takes food from an older bird.

Young falcons learn to hunt by grabbing food from their parents in midair.

MEET THE BIRDS

There more than 35 species of falcons. Let's take a look at some of them!

Peregrine Falcon
The peregrine falcon is the fastest animal in the world. When diving, this bird can hit speeds of more than 200 miles per hour (320 kph)! Peregrine falcons migrate up to 15,500 miles (25,000 km) each year.

Gyrfalcon
The world's largest falcon, the gyrfalcon, lives in far northern Arctic regions. Gyrfalcons hunt by flying low to the ground. Once they spot their prey, they chase after it, dive, and grab their meal!

American Kestrel
American kestrels are the smallest falcons in North America. Those living in the northern reaches of the continent migrate to warmer areas each winter. These falcons use their wings and tails to ride winds and hover in the air.

GLOSSARY

apex predators animals that hunt without being hunted by any other animals

female a falcon that can lay eggs

incubate to sit on eggs and keep them warm until they hatch

mate to come together to have young

prey animals that are hunted and eaten by other animals

raptor a large, strong bird with a hooked beak and large talons that eats mostly meat

stoop the act of diving down quickly to attack prey

species groups of animals that are similar and can reproduce together

talons the sharp claws of a predatory bird

translucent almost totally clear and see-through

INDEX

beaks 6, 15
chicks 18–19
eggs 16, 18
eyesight 6, 10
hunter 4, 6
mate 16
nest 16, 20
prey 4, 6, 10, 14, 22
raptor 4, 6–7, 14
speed 4, 8, 12
stoop 12
talons 6, 14
wings 4, 8–9, 12, 20, 22

READ MORE

Riggs, Kate. *Falcons (Amazing Animals).* Mankato, MN: The Creative Company, 2023.

Sommer, Nathan. *Peregrine Falcon vs. Red-Tailed Hawk (Animal Battles).* Minneapolis: Bellwether Media, 2024.

LEARN MORE ONLINE

1. Go to **FactSurfer.com** or scan the QR code below.
2. Enter "**Speedy Falcons**" into the search box.
3. Click on the cover of this book to see a list of websites.

ABOUT THE AUTHOR

Bryan Langdo has written more than 20 books for children and has illustrated plenty of others. He lives in New Jersey with his wife, two kids, three dogs, and three cats.